Louisiana Life Series, No. 9

CITY OF THE DEAD

A JOURNEY THROUGH ST. LOUIS CEMETERY #1

NEW ORLEANS, LOUISIANA

by
Robert Florence

Published by
The Center for Louisiana Studies
University of Southwestern Louisiana

Inside Cover Drawing by Rashid Levy

Library of Congress Catalog Number: 95-83197
ISBN Number: 1-887366-02-4

Copyright 1996
University of Southwestern Louisiana
Lafayette, Louisiana

Published by The Center for Louisiana Studies
P.O. Box 40831
University of Southwestern Louisiana
Lafayette, LA   70504-0831

Acknowledgments

Grateful Acknowledgments go to the Archdiocesan Cemeteries, Blue Lu Barker, Bettmann Archive, Amanda Boenitz, Warren Brazile, Center for Louisiana Studies, Jocelyn Clapp, Glenn R. Conrad, Denise Dumke, George Febres, Ivan Foley, Fraenkel Gallery, Rosemarie Gawelko, Walter Glapion, Kenny Hauck, Hal Leonard Corporation, John Henry, Historic New Orleans Collection, Jean Lafitte National Park, Jo Ann Klute, Jerah Johnson, Pat Jolly, Candy Kirby, Regina M. LaBiche, Janice Lee, Joseph Logsdon, Louisiana State Museum, Magic Tours, John Magill, Fr. Ray John Marek, Perry Mathieu, Keith Weldon Medley, Sybil Morial, Richard Rochester, Jeff Rubin, Save Our Cemeteries, A. J. Sisco, Michael P. Smith, Sally Stassi, Fr. Roger Temme, Evelyn Turner, and Warner Brothers Publications.

Special Thanks go to Michael D. Boudreaux

Part of the proceeds from this book are dedicated to the St. Louis Cemetery Preservation Fund.

For *Helene*

NOTES

GEOGRAPHICAL NOTE:

The winding, haphazard pathways of the St. Louis Cemetery #1 have been known to disorient visitors. Directions through the cemetery in this book are given as are directions throughout the city of New Orleans; geography is oriented around the river. A map of New Orleans is anything but a perfect grid. Streets disect each other at extreme angles, creating some confusing geography, and several avenues curve due to the bend of the river. Since it is often pointless to direct people north, south, east, or west, people are directed toward-the-river ("Riverside"), away-from-the-river ("Lakeside"), upriver ("Uptown"), or downriver ("Downtown"). These designations likewise apply to the maze-like St. Louis Cemetery. (A map which follows the book's suggested route is included at the end.)

"CREOLE" NOTE:

The word "Creole" is used widely in New Orleans and has many potential meanings. Chronologically it indicates Louisiana's colonial time period. For the purposes of this book, "Creole" referring to a person signifies someone born in Louisiana during the colonial (Creole) time. A Creole could be of any ethnic or national orgin (French, African, Spanish, Choctaw, German, etc.), or any mix thereof.

MUSICAL NOTE:

This book should be read to the strains of a calliope, which usually serve as a soundtrack to a St. Louis Cemetery #1 visit.

The levee along the river, site of earliest New Orleans burial.

City Of The Dead

The mysteriously enticing above-ground cemeteries of New Orleans present a profound display of mortality. However, these "cities of the dead" also invoke life. What they contain is indeed immortal. Not only do these graveyards harbor the remnants of a past which perpetually lure visitors through the gates; their compelling structures also serve as caretakers to people who have shaped and continue to shape New Orleans in every facet of life imaginable.

The oldest and most significant of these cemeteries is the St. Louis #1. To journey through this city of the dead is to journey through the city of New Orleans, past, present, and future. No single historic site or structure portrays the city's history as accurately and honestly, as vividly and poetically. A visit to this cemetery offers an examination of New Orleans culture, geology, economics, society, and law, as well as some of the city's more indescribable qualities. Consequently, many in New Orleans call the St. Louis Cemetery #1, "*THE* city of the dead."

A basic way in which this and several other above-ground cemeteries indicate the history of New Orleans is that they map out the growth of the city, chronologically pinpointing its development. The newest cemeteries were always on the settlement's very outskirts. In fact, the city's first burial site was located where New Orleans itself began—on the banks of the Mississippi River. To track the growth of New Orleans, one must start at the river. The story of New Orleans burial begins here as well, on the natural levee.

"Levee," derived from the French verb "lever"/to raise, means "raised." This word describes the condition of riverside land, explaining why, in an area mostly below sea level, people chose to bury there. (Moreover, this raised land accounts for the location of the French Quarter itself, on relatively dry ground rather than in the surrounding swamp.) The earliest burials took place along the banks of the river, for that is where the highest and best-drained land existed, and still exists.

New Orleans is situated in a delta, wherein the land has been created from flooding. Before effective flood control, moving bodies of water would overflow their banks annually and deposit sediment drained from throughout North America. (The Mississippi River alone drains more than one million square miles.) Consequently, the closer to the river, the higher the land, which descends in altitude as it tapers away toward the area once known as the "Back of Town."

The same flooding which created New Orleans has always endangered the city. Despite the current widespread presence of water pumping stations, control structures, spillways, jetties, and revetments, Mother Nature can still wreak havoc. On May 8, 1995, 18 inches of rain fell in 6 hours, killing several people and doing seven hundred and sixty million dollars worth of damage. (Addressing disgruntled New Orleans residents in the wake of this flood, Sewage and Water Board executive director Harold Gorman explained: "The first problem is history: [1st French Colonial Governor] Bienville made a mistake when he landed here."[1])

The combination of high rainfall and low altitude also poses a severe challenge to burial, and the Crescent City's first inhabitants quickly discovered this dilemma. Imagine what would happen to bouyant, wooden caskets buried in the levee as the water table rose: A hard rain would push them back up above the ground. It is difficult to bury "six feet under" in a city much of which is itself "six feet under." Faced with the potential for saturated caskets to break apart during a flood and send human remains down the sloped streets of the city, the first New Orleanians were soon to curtail the practice of riverside burial.

"At high tide, the river flows through the streets. The subsoil is swampy. New Orleans becomes famous for its tombs . . . "[2]

-A History of Regional Growth

In The Beginning:
The Saint Peter Street Cemetery

In 1721, three years after the founding of New Orleans, Royal Engineer Adrien de Pauger created the first plan of the city. Today's military grid pattern of French Quarter streets follows that same design. A cemetery was included in the first plan. Considering that caskets did not always stay below ground and that the riverside burial ground sloped into the Vieux Carré, this first cemetery was placed outside the limits of the city (on the "upriver"/west side of St. Peter St., between today's Burgundy and Rampart streets). If caskets were to emerge from this below-ground cemetery, they would now be washed away from the city towards an uninhabited swamp.

The Saint Peter Street Cemetery became the city's first cemetery, circa 1725, and the first cemetery to mark the city's outermost edge. It was believed that nothing remained from this cemetery until April of 1984, when coffins and bones were uncovered on this site during excavation for a condominium. Research by Louisiana State University archeologists showed that both blacks and whites were buried in the city's first cemetery. (The St. Louis Cemetery also buried people of both races from the beginning. Although uncommon in former American slave-holding areas, cemeteries and churches of early New Orleans did not discriminate along racial lines.) Other than these bones, the only other St. Peter Street Cemetery relics could be bricks now found in the St. Louis Cathedral, possibly taken from the walls of this first cemetery.

(Other eighteenth century New Orleans cemeteries existed at the following locations: behind the St. Louis Cathedral; adjacent to the Ursuline Convent; at Congo Square; on the block bounded by Bienville, Chartres, Conti and Royal Streets; and at the corners of Royal and Barracks and Esplanade and Dauphine.)

Little remains from the St. Peter Street Cemetery. For that matter, virtually no structures remain from New Orleans' French period. (The Ursuline Convent and the reconstructed Madame John's Legacy are two exceptions.) The French Quarter today looks nothing like it did during the French colonial period. The French settlement was largely built of wood, which is why French Colonial architecture no longer exists in the French Quarter. Two fires destroyed most of the French settlement in the late 1700s, wiping the slate clean for the Spanish administration to create for all practical purposes a new city.

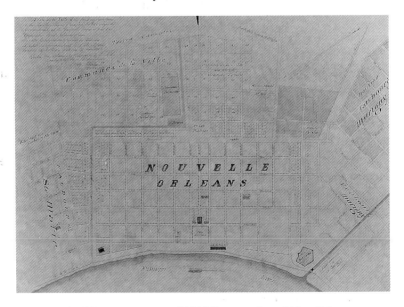

1755 Thierry plan of New Orleans, 1st cemetery depicted below St. Peter
Street. Courtesy Historic New Orleans Collection

1870s d'Hemecourt copy of 1812 Tanesse plan of New Orleans.
Cimetière Catholique noted at site of St. Louis Cemetery #1.
Carondelet Canal ending at turning basin on Congo Square.
Courtesy Historic New Orleans Collection

As a result, much of what constitutes "French Quarter architecture" was actually introduced when Louisiana was a Spanish colony, such as plaster-over-brick, iron work, balconies, tile roofs, and courtyards. The St. Louis Cemetery tombs are made from the same brick covered with plaster, and above-ground burial itself, in the form of wall vaults, was also introduced by the Spanish. The cemetery is therefore another example of Spanish success in physically creating a lasting city where the French failed. Like most of the oldest of structures in New Orleans, the City of the Dead dates to the Spanish period, following the first great fire. However, French ideas of design and style, particularly the influence of architect J. N. B. de Pouilly, ultimately determined the cemetery's highest aesthetic achievements and its general appearance, attained in the nineteenth century.

It is not surprising that the St. Louis Cemetery #1 was established in 1789 when one considers what occurred the year before. In 1788 the first great fire destroyed 80 percent of the city (852 wooden, French Colonial buildings). There was also a flood and an epidemic, resulting in a high mortality rate which would overcrowd the Saint Peter Street Cemetery. By that year the city itself had grown out to Rampart Street. The next cemetery, St. Louis #1, would once again be placed outside the limits of the city, on the other side of Rampart Street, due to a belief that proximity to cemeteries would enhance the dreaded epidemics of lethal diseases.

The journey to the St. Louis Cemetery #1 begins by crossing Rampart Street. However, the first structure one encounters is the city's oldest surviving church, Our Lady of Guadalupe, which, like the cemetery itself, exists as a result of death and burial practice.

The Mortuary Chapel

In 1826, St. Anthony's Church (now known as Our Lady of Guadalupe) was built as a mortuary chapel. The cemeteries had already been placed outside the limits of the city twice owing to fear of contagion, but by the early nineteenth century yellow fever and malaria had become so devastating that the Board of Health forbade the church from having funeral services in St. Louis Cathedral. Authorities believed that transporting dead bodies from the Cathedral through the City streets to the cemetery would spread disease. As a result, the Church established this mortuary chapel between Rampart Street and the cemetery. It was used for funerals, primarily of yellow fever victims. There the services were conducted and the caskets then borne out the back because the St. Louis Cemetery #1 was located directly behind the church.

Yet when exiting the chapel today you no longer immediately find tombs, but rather Basin Street. In 1795, six years after the establishment of the cemetery, the Spanish dug the Carondelet Canal, linking Bayou St. John to the city. (This canal was supposed to extend up Basin St. to "Canal" St. and connect with the Mississippi River. This connection did not happen, and Canal St. became one of a number of New Orleans streets named for something which never existed.) To facilitate commerce, a turning basin was created farther down the street, closer to Congo Square, hence the name Basin St. The earliest section of the cemetery then became a road for a navigation company, and later the site of a railroad line. The front section of the cemetery was then closed to burial and the central section became the front. Therefore when you pass through the gate, you are treading on what was once the cemetery's middleground.

The Mortuary Chapel

Storyville

"Basin St., that's the street, where all the ghosts from Storyville and the St. Louis Cemetery meet . . ."[3]

-Dr. John

The sign reading "Basin St." causes many cemetery visitors to ponder the early days of Jazz, New Orleans Jazz. The inspiration is appropriate, for here you are a stone's throw from the former "Storyville," the infamous turn-of-the-century New Orleans red-light district. Contrary to popular belief, Jazz was not born in Storyville, yet it certainly gained much momentum there. Moreover, this neighborhood would give Traditional Jazz a degree of mystique above and beyond any other neighborhood in any other city, anywhere. At the very least, Storyville was a unique legal and social experiment, unparalleled in United States history, resulting from a long history of prostitution in New Orleans.

Prostitution was part of New Orleans from the beginning, a result of the fact that many of the city's first female colonists were prostitutes. The French government had a difficult time getting people to leave their comfortable Mediterranean country to come to a virtually unhabitable

Basin Street

8

Aerial photograph, circa 1914. St. Louis Cemeteries #1 & #2 delineate Storyville. Mortuary Chapel stands bottom right. Courtesy Historic New Orleans Collection.

swamp where one's survival chances were not great. Louisiana offered flooding, mosquito swarms, hurricanes, venemous reptiles, and tropical fevers in abundance. On the site of Basin St. three hundred years ago you would have found yourself up to your knees in mud and water throughout much of the year. Perhaps the most telling fact is that Native Americans, who had been in the region for thousands of years and were well-adapted to the challenging environment, chose not to live here. (In many ways New Orleans is still an unlikely place to situate a city.) To overcome the lack of appeal to potential colonists, the French resorted to kidnapping people off streets, and ultimately emptying out prisons. Female houses of detention contributed many convicted prostitutes to the emigrating ships.

During the colonial, or "Creole," era, prostitution as a business did not thrive, partly because concubines were an entrenched part of society. Creole men, primarily aristocrats, would keep mistresses, as part of the tradition known as "placage." (This word is derived from the French verb "placer"/to place, in that these women were "placed" in provided homes.) The miscegenation of placage gave rise to the "quadroon" and "octaroon" mistress. Following the Louisiana Purchase, a more puritanical American morality would find this type of concubinage scandalous and offensive. When American New Orleans brought the curtain down on placage, the demand for prostitution skyrocketed.

Aerial view of Storyville, 1906. Cemetery can be seen far right.
Courtesy Historic New Orleans Collection.

Another even larger factor behind the increase in prostitution was tied to the Louisiana Purchase—the boom in shipping. Louisiana had just been a French and Spanish colony, with New Orleans a relatively sleepy outpost, trading primarily with France and Spain. The United States lifted trade restrictions, creating an international seaport, and shipping boomed. Naturally prostitution did as well.

Throughout the nineteenth century, red-light districts sprung up throughout the city. Distressed over real estate value, property owners pressured the city to take action. Alderman Sidney Story came up with an ordinance addressing the issue, which was passed in 1897. Story knew that the city fathers could not eliminate prostitution, but believed it could be controlled by being confined to one supervised area. So the city chose an already-existing red-light district (they did not need to go out and create one), the three blocks along Basin Street and four blocks extending back to North Robertson Street. Story's ordinance turned this section into a district of decriminalized prostitution and gaming, and the press ironically named it "Storyville." Story did not find this amusing but his plan worked. Other red-light districts disappeared and in general crime in New Orleans decreased.

Yet a legitimized zone of ill-repute did not sit well with many people, and there were those working to close Storyville. The District became history in 1917, by order of the United States Department of the Navy. That year the United States entered World War I, and with so many ships leaving from New Orleans, the Navy concluded that Storyville would be a bad influence on its sailors.

"Storyville . . . was closed by the United States Department of the Navy, the federal government having decreed in effect, that only illegal prostitution was to be practiced in the vicinity of it's military installations."

-Al Rose, "Storyville"[4]

Some people find Storyville's legal aspects fascinating. Others fixate on the sins of the flesh committed from crib to mansion. But it seems that most people today associate Storyville with music. Basin Street's high-brow, ornate bordellos employed genius piano players, and dance halls throughout the district hired the hottest of bands, participating in the genesis of Jazz.

A veritable roll call of New Orleans Jazz pioneers, such as Buddy Bolden, King Oliver, Jelly Roll Morton, Tony Jackson, Sidney Bechet, Paul Barbarin, Kid Ory, Freddy Keppard, Bunk Johnson, Henry "Red" Allen,

Manuel Perez, and several others, played the parlors and gin joints during that twenty-year period, leading bands, many on a regular basis. It is believed that the word "Jazz" may have originated in Storyville and other such red-light districts, in that some people initially called it "Jezebel" music. "Jezebel" turned to "Jez," and "Jez" became "Jazz". . .

Many visitors to New Orleans seek out remaining structures from the Storyville district, but its buildings were mostly destroyed in the late 1930s to make way for the Iberville housing project. In a sense, the tombs of the St. Louis Cemetery are the only structures that remain from Storyville. Yet the cemetery had been around a century before Sidney Story's legislation was passed and still stands long after the closing of the district. Crossing Basin Street, you arrive at the border of Storyville's ghost town, and the entrance to the City of the Dead.

1834 John Latrobe Watercolor of St. Louis Cemetery, #1, when the Varney tomb was in the middle. Courtesy Historic New Orleans Collection.

Entrance to City of the Dead

The Cemetery

Upon entering the City of the Dead, the first structure you come upon is the pyramid-shaped Varney tomb, which is of Egyptian Revival Style architecture. Although the Varney tomb once stood in the middle of the cemetery, it is appropriate that the cemetery now begins with this tomb, for not only does Egyptian design represent a spectacular funerary tradition, it indicates permanence.

Much like the streets of New Orleans, the erratic rows of the cemetery display a number of architectural styles, including Greek, Egyptian, Baroque, and Gothic Revival. In *Life On The Mississippi* Mark Twain wrote, "There is no architecture in New Orleans, except in the cemeteries."[5] New Orleans has always placed enormous value upon architectural detail, and some of the city's most exacting craftsmanship is found in the stone of the cemetery's monuments. Many of the most skilled sculptors in the era before the Civil War were free people of color.

Varney Tomb

A severe land shortage has characterized South Louisiana throughout its history. New Orleans was practically an island, surrounded by water on all sides, until A. Baldwin Wood's water pumps were installed by the early twentieth century. This lack of liveable space is reflected in the city's layout. For example, throughout Uptown New Orleans there are hundreds of enormous homes right next to one another. (Likewise, in the cemetery, notice the narrow passages between tombs.) If the wealthiest people of the city, which when their homes were built was one of the wealthiest cities in the world, could not afford big yards, it stands to reason that one does not find rolling meadows through the cemeteries.

The City of the Dead is therefore crowded like New Orleans itself, and to further save land, above-ground tombs have been used over and over

again. In the near future, people will not be buried below ground horizontally, one-person-per-grave. There is simply no longer enough room to continue this practice. Yet in New Orleans, people have been buried in an efficient, economical manner for more than two hundred years. An exploration of St. Louis Cemetery is an examination of this multiple, above-ground burial, of which there are three basic types.

All three types of multiple burial have one thing in common: an ordinance which states that "a year and a day" is the minimum amount of time for which a casket must remain entombed. That is the minimum amount of time determined necessary for a corpse to fully decompose. (However, if the corpse has not sufficiently broken down after a year and a day, the following "multiple burial" is put off until a later date.) That does not sound like much time, but when above-ground burial was brought into New Orleans, the rate at which corpses decomposed was naturally more rapid due to a general absence of embalming. During most of this cemetery's busiest decades, embalming was not practiced, and would not become commonplace until the late nineteenth century.

Today, due to water pumps draining New Orleans, it is possible to bury below the ground. Yet even in the case of below-ground burial, a tradition tied to this historical lack of embalming persists: New Orleans burials tend to happen quickly, often within twenty-four to forty-eight hours of the time of death.

In an increasingly homogenized society, New Orleans is a city which exuberantly upholds its unique traditions, including rituals of burial. The Jazz Funeral is an excellent example of this. It is interesting to note that even after the land was drained and New Orleans acquired the ability to bury below ground, people overwhelmingly stuck with the established tradition of above-ground burial.

Equally significant is the fact that in a region devoid of stone, the marble and granite were mainly imported for use in the cemeteries. It is rare to find a stone building in the French Quarter, Garden District, or other historic neighborhoods of the living, yet throughout the cities of the dead exquisite creations in stone dazzle the senses.

Many visitors to the city find the above-ground nature of the tombs strange, if not unnerving. This regional distinction is of course the result of geology. Before New Orleans had the ability to drain land with pumps, below-ground burial was very challenging. Another unique aspect of local burial is also determined by geology—the fact that most tombs have been used several times.

Wall Vault

Types of Burial

The Wall Vault:

The first type of multiple, above-ground tomb encountered is that which forms a boundary between the City of the Dead and the City of New Orleans—the wall vault. These serve as the walls of the cemetery. To entomb in a wall vault, you must remove the marble plaque, which is held in place by a long metal screw and /or caulked in. Then the layer of brick and plaster behind the plaque is broken down. The casket within is then removed and disposed of. During the nineteenth century the used caskets were burned for fear of contagion. Today they are simply thrown away. (Discarded caskets have been known to raise eyebrows. Recently a visitor to the city became extremely panicked in the Lafayette Cemetery because he claimed to have seen "a casket sticking out of a dumpster!"; he also had an Anne Rice novel sticking out of his back pocket.)

Any human remains found in the old casket are placed back in the vault, not burned. This being a Catholic cemetery, cremation was forbidden. The human remains of the earlier entombment are then pushed to the side or rear, making room for the next coffin. Therefore, in the recesses of the wall vaults there lie successive generations of mingled remains.

Wall vaults are also called "oven vaults." One reason is that their barrel vault shape suggests old brick baker's ovens. More significantly, these brick vaults act like ovens. A year and a day would not be sufficient time in cooler latitudes for a corpse to fully decompose. But if a sealed casket is placed into a South Louisiana wall vault between the months of May and September, the deceased is subjected to temperatures in the hundreds of degrees Farenheit. This usually results in accelerated decomposition.

The region's geology is vividly reflected in the wall vaults. Walking down the first aisle you can see the entire bank of vaults leaning inward, and that the entire bottom row has sunk more than halfway. Slightly leaning and sunken, much like many New Orleans structures built for the living.

The Family/Private Tomb:

Across the path from the wall vaults you find the second type of multiple, above-ground burial—family tombs. These are owned and used by specific families. That is not to say that wall vaults do not house families. They usually do, yet wall vaults were often not owned. As is the case in cities of the living, families with less money tended to rent smaller

17

Sunken Bottom Row

dwellings. (As is also the case in a city of the living, if the rent is not paid, occupants could be evicted.) Wall vaults would also be rented to family tomb owners as temporary resting places when a tomb was full and more than one family member died within a year and a day.

However, family tombs are not rented. The family purchases the plot of land, the same as in a real estate deal for new home construction, and builds the tomb on it according to their needs, personal taste, and budget. Some family tombs have three or four vaults; some have one. Most have two. The top vault is used first, then the remains are moved down until the tomb is full. After a year-and-a-day one can remove the remains from the bottom and transfer them to the *caveau*, a chamber in the tomb's foundation. It is unlikely that the *caveau* would ever run out of room, for bones do break down rather quickly.

Family Tombs

The *caveau* can therefore house countless branches of a family tree. Louisiana law has seen to it that these branches proliferate within the tomb. Under a legal principle known as "forced heirship," parents are legally bound to leave their estates to their children. Estates naturally include family tombs.

Family tombs mirror the old townhouses and shotguns which shelter living New Orleans families. First of all, they are proportionally tall, narrow, and long. And during the nineteenth century when more residences were used by one family and when the St. Louis #1 tombs were being used much more frequently, the city's houses and tombs simultaneously sheltered large extended families, with it's many members all living together.

> "Whether they were simple or elaborate, early Louisiana homes filled a function that, like their actual buildings, has been lost. Home was the center of the family's existence and physical maintenance - not simply for parents and their children but often for several generations under one roof."[6]
>
> -Norman Ferachi & Sue Eakin

A few short steps down the path reveal several ways in which the structures inside the cemetery mirror those of the larger city. There are the plaster-covered brick buildings, materials introduced by the Spanish. There are fences which surround the structures, forming complete protective enclosures, and lockable gates which swing open at the entrance to the tomb. And of course the iron work, the many, many styles and motifs of exquisite iron work, a signature of the city of New Orleans. The tombs furthermore seem to become windowless microcosms of buildings with the addition of drain gutters, and even chimneys (which serve as decorative vents).

Continuing down the row you notice that the parallels do not end with the structures themselves. Between the tombs and on the shoulders of the paths are strewn thousands of white clam shells, which you also can find on New Orleans driveways and along the shoulders of South Louisiana roads. With no stone indigenous to the region, these native shells are used as gravel. You also find sweet olive trees which provide the cemetery with a pungent sweet fragrance during their bloom cycle. Fragrant plant life has historically been brought into New Orleans to cover foul smells.

The town has always been riddled with disgusting odors, which have not always been from the vomit encrusted on Bourbon Street. There is decomposing organic matter below the ground emitting smells that were

Ornate iron fence
with swinging gate

Drain gutter

"Chimney"

Clam shells

once mistaken for deadly "miasmas." And during colonial times the streets were basically open sewers. Residents dumped chamber pots into the unpaved streets. Add kitchen refuse and animal carcasses to the 95 degree temperatures, 100 percent humidity, six feet of annual rainfall, and a high water table, and it is little wonder that people spent most of their time back in the courtyards, or that fragrant plant life was introduced. Sweet-smelling blossoms also made more bearable the cemeteries crowded with unembalmed, decomposing bodies in vented tombs.

Accompanying the tombs you can find cast-iron benches, which were popularized in the mid 1800s. In nineteenth-century New Orleans mourning was an intense tradition. People would spend long hours visiting their family tombs and the cemeteries got crowded, particularly on religious holidays. The church consequently provided these iron benches for the thousands of visitors. People in New Orleans then began to associate them with cemeteries and began to call the benches "cemetery furniture." Some believe that the popularity of these accessories spread from New Orleans but that it was difficult to market them elsewhere with the name "cemetery furniture." Consequently, people in other places opted for a less morbid-sounding name, like "patio furniture." Whether that claim is true or not, some New Orleanians still call such benches "cemetery furniture."

The cemetery furniture was well-travelled, particularly on All Saints Day, as is described in the novel *Interview With A Vampire*:

> It is the day in New Orleans when all the faithful go to the cemeteries to care for the graves of their loved ones. They whitewash the plaster walls of the vaults, clean the names cut into the marble slabs. And finally they deck the tomb with flowers. In the St. Louis Cemetery . . . there were even little iron benches before the graves where the families might sit to receive the other families who had come to the cemetery for the same purpose.[7]
>
> -Anne Rice

After passing several tombs, you can recognize a widely encompassing trait shared between the City of the Dead and New Orleans: in one instant structures vary from profoundly decrepit to lavishly perfect. Just as the character of New Orleans' neighborhoods can change from block to block, the tone of a street often varies from building to building. The same may be said for the St. Louis Cemetery #1; you can pass one dilapidated heap of a tomb after another and suddenly come across a grave that glistens. (Many of these tombs have a plaque which reads "Perpetual Care," a fund established with the Archdiocese that maintains the tomb.)

A fragrant Sweet Olive Tree blooms above stepped
tombs which have settled below sea level.

Cemetery Furniture

Arriving at the first corner, uptown riverside (southwest), you have a rare view of the cemetery. The brick wall on the other side, towards the lake, marks the end of the cemetery. (The cemetery used to extend past that point.) Since the path is straight and unobstructed, you can see from one side of the cemetery to the other, a rarity in the St. Louis #1. For example, if you look back in the other direction, downriver, towards Congo Square, you do not see the other side. The path veers to the right and tombs obstruct the view.

Some visitors find this trait to be the most interesting aspect of the cemetery. In contrast to so many American cemeteries, the St. Louis #1 is not a neatly arranged grid pattern. It is much more of a labrynth. An aerial photograph clearly demonstrates this characteristic. Note that the "paths" do not usually go very far, or that they veer off at strange angles.

This curious geography exists because the cemetery, like New Orleans itself, was not laid out with a master plan, but piecemeal, as land was being reclaimed. New Orleans' streets also slice up the city map at odd and extreme angles. In the cemetery, a new tomb could easily be built on what was yesterday's path. And during yellow fever and malaria epidemics, when 10 percent of the city's population could be wiped out in a matter of months, little thought was given to the cemetery's overall configuration; it was all the church could do to build the tombs and inter the thousands of infected corpses. As do the Mississippi-River-bend-tangled streets of New Orleans, the paths of the cemetery come at one another from strange, severe angles, creating a real maze. This becomes quite apparent walking through the middle of the cemetery.

The Stepped Tomb:

Getting off the straight path and into this labrynth, you start to see a type of burial which is neither multiple nor always fully above-ground: the "stepped tomb," so called for its ridges up the sides or on the top which resemble steps. There are many types, the most basic being a low-lying grave with "stepped" sides ascending to a flat top. The stepped tomb probably originates from an ancient burial technique in which the corpse was simply laid on the ground and covered with earth. In constructing the stepped tomb a low foundation of brick is laid and the coffin placed on top. After the church service bricks are assembled in a pyramid shape over the casket.

These graves are used only once, and therefore do not need a *caveau* in which to place many generations of decomposed remains. This chamber adds stability in the form of weight distribution. Lacking this stability, stepped tombs sink the most rapidly. You can see them at varying levels of submergence throughout the cemetery. Some are all the way gone, leaving only a path-like, flat layer of brick on the ground. The church will not bury on top of a sunken tomb. (Sunken tombs create gaps among the rows of tombs, contributing to the cemetery's irregular design.)

The stepped-tomb is obviously not the ideal form of internment. However, the most efficient procedure is found in the third type of multiple, above-ground burial: the Society Tomb.

Stepped tomb

Society Tombs

The aftermath of death can be very expensive, and New Orleans' above-ground cemetery burial is more costly than most. Considering that the tombs house infinite generations, this is a significant investment. And since the finest of nineteenth century artisans and craftsmen serviced the cities of the dead, prices could be astronomical. To cut costs, people would band together in "Benevolent Associations." These societies would reduce medical bills and help support widows, but their main purpose was to provide a sort of burial insurance, ensuring interment in a consecrated cemetery. Members were buried in the multi-vaulted "society tombs". Benevolent societies could be comprised of people practicing the same trade, members of a religious order, veterans, or through various other common interests, but many of the St. Louis Cemetery #1's Society Tombs house immigrant groups. During the nineteenth century, New Orleans was, following New York City, the largest U. S. port of entry for immigration. Prodigious immigration is clearly reflected in the St. Louis Cemetery.

Society tombs dominate the City of the Dead's skyline, and the most striking is the Italian Mutual Benevolent Society tomb. Architecturally exquisite, and the cemetery's tallest structure, its building material is also worthy of attention. The entire facade is made of marble imported from Italy. Importing marble was more expensive than having it quarried in the United States, but many immigrant groups did this to show an allegiance to their heritage. Speaking of expense, this tomb was built in 1857 at a price of $40,000.

Not only was the Italian Society tomb's marble imported, the sculptor was as well. Pietro Gualdi was brought to New Orleans to design this monument and spent the rest of his life in the Crescent City. This may be the only instance known of a tomb being responsible for a person emigrating across an ocean never to return to his native country. Gualdi was the first person to be buried in his masterpiece.

With twenty-four vaults, this edifice is one of the cemetery's largest. Its caveau is on the interior, a massive cylinder which can easily hold thousands of remains. Consider that within a century nearly 2,400 people—the headcount of a decent-sized cemetery in many other places—could conceivably be buried in this one tomb, and the efficiency of land usage in this burial practice becomes apparent.

Italian Society Tomb

Easy Rider

The Italian Society tomb gained much notoriety when it appeared in the film *Easy Rider*. This movie tells the story of Captain America (Peter Fonda) and Billy (Dennis Hopper) on a Harley Davidson-borne pilgrammage across country to the New Orleans Mardi Gras. Amidst the pandemonium of Carnival, they go to a brothel and from there bring two prostitutes into the St. Louis Cemetery. They all take L.S.D., and the ensuing meltdown is one of the most memorable, and notorious, scenes executed in the history of American film-making.

Their hallucinogenic rampage through the cemetery begins playfully enough, but leads to multiple bad trips. One of the girls finds herself naked in a sunken tomb with Captain America and is shortly thereafter crouching over a grave screaming that she is going to die, while Billy forces himself upon the other girl between two tombs. Meanwhile Peter Fonda's character winds up crawling all over the "Italia" statue, crying his eyes out, seeming to have mistaken the statue for his mother.

Yet the frenzied montage of non-sequitorial images becomes difficult to comprehend, with a psychedelic soundtrack in the background, interspliced with scenes from some sort of unexplained surrealistic funeral and droning voices reciting the Apostle's Creed, Hail Mary, and Our Father. The pandemonium seems to culminate with Dennis Hopper's character raping the girl between the tombs as the other one proclaims, "I'm dead."

"Easy Rider" was a profoundly popular film in 1969. Millions saw it, and people with family tombs in the St. Louis Cemetery paid particularly close attention to that cemetery scene. Many were shocked that it was filmed on a property owned by the Church.

It turns out that the film crew did not get a permit to shoot this sequence, and as a result of complaints from tomb owners, "Easy Rider" was the last major motion picture ever filmed in the City of the Dead. The Archdiocese no longer allows filming in the cemetery, except in the case of select, approved documentaries and educational films. "Easy Rider" definitely complicated things for most subsequent film makers interested in using this City of the Dead.

Perhaps this film also got a bad rap from a rumor that Dennis Hopper yanked the missing heads off of the headless "Charity" statue. Though Hopper appears capable of doing so in the aforementioned scene, those heads are gone due to vandalism. It should not be surprising that there is vandalism in the cemetery. It is more surprising that there is not more

Headless statue of Charity

vandalism. The endurance of these tombs could very well translate into a respect for, if not a fear of, the dead.

Many of the burial societies no longer exist. Case in point, the Italian Society Tomb has not been used in years. Of the relatively few burials which take place in the St. Louis #1, most are in family tombs or wall vaults. Across from the Italian Tomb you find the only society tomb still in use, that of the former Portuguese Society. It is no longer a resting place for deceased Portuguese, but rather a St. Vincent de Paul Society tomb, which provides free burial for the poor. The only other society tomb to have been used recently is the second Portuguese Society Tomb, which accommodated Vietnamese refugees in the 1970s.

Society tombs house people of diverse orgin. The Dieu Nous Protege Society tomb contains people of African descent. The Cervantes Society tomb was established by Spanish New Orleanians. A few rows from it is a Chinese society tomb. The largest society tomb is that of the French. And an amalgam of New Orleans heritage and history is embodied in the Orleans Battalion of Artillery society tomb, a monument to veterans of the Battle of New Orleans.

Former Portuguese Society Tomb

Second Portuguese Society Tomb

Dieu Nous Protege Society Tomb: final resting place for free people of color

Cervantes Society Tomb
Graves of Spanish immigrants

Chinese Society Tomb

French Society Tomb, the largest in the cemetery, with an entire wing for children.

Battle of New Orleans

The Battle of New Orleans was the final battle of the War of 1812, a war which for the first time would establish the United States as a military power only thirty years into the nation's history. The battle was a turning point in New Orleans history, for the Louisiana Purchase had just occurred and New Orleanians did not want to be considered "Americans" for several different cultural reasons. Yet after a successful repulsion of British forces with the help of U. S. troops, New Orleans began to feel more at home in the United States. This battle's diversity of troops makes for some fascinating military history.

The federal government sent Andrew Jackson to command federal troops. (The success of this battle would gain Jackson popularity which led to the presidency.) Locally, an eclectic array of Creoles would contribute. The troops included many New Orleanians of French descent, as well as foreign-born French. There were two battalions of free people of color, led by free black officers. (People of African descent, both slave and free, had been fighting in Louisiana since the 1730s. These battalions had black line officers starting in the 1770s.) Pirates contributed, namely Jean Lafitte and his "Baratarians." There were Choctaw Indians (led by Major Pierre Jugeant, of Choctaw descent and raised among Native Americans), Spanish Creoles, and recent émigrés forced to leave the Caribbean due to Haitian independence.

The Battle of New Orleans
Courtesy The Historic New Orleans Collection

Although much of this diverse militia had little military experience, it would defeat the world's greatest military power, the British Navy. This was accomplished by the U. S. forces building a 600 yard long rampart and hiding behind it. Sent into this line of fire were the British troops, wearing bright red coats, with fife and drum corps playing. It was a decisive victory: more than 2000 British casualties with only 71 on the other side of that rampart. Ironically, the treaty ending the war had been signed in Belgium three weeks before the battle, but without telephones and fax machines, word would not make it across the ocean in time.

This society tomb's vaults house veterans of the battle, their iron tablets bearing symbols of mourning and triumph. Inverted torches stand for death (In the Roman Coliseum, if a torch was turned upside down, somebody was going to die.), whereas the wreath symbolizes victory. In the corner of the plates you find flaming mortar shells. Models of the mortar shells sit atop models of the cannons which played a big role in the American victory. Suspended by these cannons are anchor chains. But perhaps the most interesting image on the tomb is the hourglass with wings attached. It stands for the passage of time, but many people in New Orleans interpret is as, "Time flies while you're having fun . . ."

The Battle of New Orleans was a successful effort on the part of many different peoples. And just as the City of New Orleans is a study of these many different people, so is the City of the Dead.

Society Tomb for veterans
of the Battle of New Orleans

The People

New Orleans is a city of interesting and odd street names. Likewise, dynamic striking names mark the "streets" of the City of the Dead. People such as Aurelia Populus, Eulalie Harang, Hyppolite Gilly, Bathilde Narcisse Alva, Henry Henry, Blanche Santa Cruz, Adeleyda Elena Feliciana Martina Leonard, Marie Minerva Monk, Anna Dupre Power Arcement, Baby Gladys Schwab, and Emilia Toutant Beauregard Belly, bear their names on plaques of marble and granite for visitors to peruse. Even at surface level, there is a strong sense that the St. Louis Cemetery #1 is home to many significant and curious people as well as to those whose stories have been forgotten. Every walk of New Orleans life finds shelter here.

New Orleans is not only a city of architecture, music, and food, but is as strongly characterized by its people. Visitors constantly remark that the residents are its most compelling, if not appealing, aspect. This cemetery contains a wide cross section of the city's population. It is also a "Who's Who" of New Orleans history, with no shortage of nationally significant historic figures. To walk through this cemetery is to walk through the human history of New Orleans.

Homer Adolph Plessy (1862-1925)

"In 1896 New Orleans shoemaker Homer Plessy asked the Supreme Court whether the U. S. Constitution meant what it said - and he lost."[8]

-Keith Weldon Medley

Past the midpoint of the cemetery, across from the Conti Street wall, you find the tomb of New Orleanian Homer Plessy. He was the plaintiff in the landmark 1896 Supreme Court case, *Plessy* v. *Ferguson*, whose decision established the precedent of "separate-but-equal," a ruling not overturned until *Brown* v. *Board of Education*. The impetus behind this far-reaching milestone in United States history finds its roots in Louisiana's unique legal system.

Louisiana law is different from that of the other forty-nine states in that it is based on French civil law, not British common law. New Orleans' legal procedure was most influenced by Roman law and the Napoleonic Code. A principle difference is that civil law bases legal decisions upon codes, as opposed to the common law practice of using established legal precedent. Colonial Louisiana drew up codes which at that time had no real parallel in American law.

34

One of the most far-reaching codes in distinguishing Louisiana from the rest of the United States was the "Code Noir," the Black Code, which addresses slavery and race. Many of the Code's articles were brutal and severe, but some established a relatively more relaxed environment in terms of slavery.

For example, a slave could sue an owner for abuse. Slaves also had the right to an education, and they could hire out their skills. Families of slaves were not separated through sale. The church baptized slave children and recognized slave marriages. It was much easier for a slave to purchase freedom, and free people of color could own property and run businesses anywhere in the city. Free blacks attended churches and patronized theatres,

Homer Plessy Tomb

and they established their own schools and social institutions. Likewise, the cemeteries were not segregated. These conditions combined with a much higher degree of racial mixing rendered early New Orleans notably different from most of slave-holding America.

Following the Louisiana Purchase, the legal system clamped down on people of African descent. Laws were passed limiting the emancipation of slaves and restricting the free people of color. After the Civil War there was great potential for change in the Reconstruction Acts, which gave blacks the right to vote. In New Orleans, Creole activists formed the Citizens Committee ("Comité des Citoyens") to register voters. However, on the heels of Reconstruction Jim Crow laws would soon arrive.

In 1890, Louisiana passed a law requiring separate railroad cars for blacks and whites, a law that the Citizens Committee would challenge. They won their first case. Homer Plessy served as the plaintiff in the more significant second case. Plessy, one-eighth black, boarded a train and sat in the white section. Light-skinned, he probably could have passed for white, which would demonstrate how arbitrary and ludicrous the law was.

Informing the conductor that he was legally Negro, Plessy was arrested. His case went to the Supreme Court in 1896 and was decided against him. This decision's precedent transcended railroad cars and went into every aspect of American public life, the most notorious being the classroom. Not until 1954 did *Brown* v. *Board of Education* render null and void the doctrine of "separate but equal," though in many ways this issue is far from resolved, as much in New Orleans as anywhere in the country.

Although *Plessy* v. *Ferguson* has been referred to as "the capstone of the arch of tyranny,"[9] it ultimately effected forward change. In *Creole New Orleans: Race and Americanization*, historians Joseph Logsdon and Caryn Cossé Bell point out that the case produced dissent used to revive Reconstruction amendments in subsequent Supreme Court decisions. Many people believe that the Civil Rights movement actually began with Homer Plessy and the Citizens Committee. It is hardly surprising, considering not only the social and cultural but also the legal history of New Orleans, that this city gave rise to the Plessy case.

> A strain of creole radicalism, more assertive and independent, with broader horizons and self-confidence, emerged to challenge American racial conceptions and the imposition of Jim Crow. It was no accident that Homer Plessy came from New Orleans and not Charleston.[10]
>
> Arnold Hirsch & Joseph Logsdon

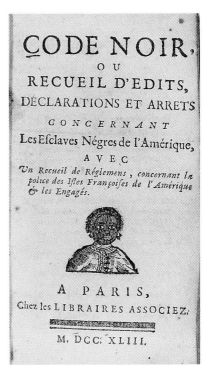

Code Noir: The Black Code, legal policy under French Civil Law regarding slavery. Courtesy Historic New Orleans Collection

Freed slaves registering to vote in New Orleans during Reconstruction
Courtesy the Bettmann Archive

Decorative Iron Work

Decorative Iron Work

Bernard de Marigny
Courtesy Louisiana State Museum

Bernard De Marigny (1788-1871)

"The last of the Creole aristocracy . . . One who knows how to dispose of a great fortune with contemptuous indifference."[11]

-Obituary of Bernard de Marigny

Down the row from Homer Plessy lies Bernard de Marigny. He embodied the nineteenth-century New Orleans ideal of the aristocratic Creole (although there are still numerous conflicting definitions of this word.) His family owned much of what is now New Orleans. The "Marigny" section, on the downriver side of the French Quarter, had been their plantation. The area of the present-day city of Mandeville was added to their estate when Bernard tried to create a "Fontainebleau on the Pontchartrain."

At age fifteen Bernard received an inheritance of millions. He was sent to Europe to be educated and to try his hand at business. Successful at neither, Marigny returned, and was subsequently credited with introducing the game of "craps" into the United States. He loved to gamble, but was not very good at it himself. The commemorative plaque on his tomb states that he "lost most of his wealth before his death;" a noteworthy comment in that he had been known as "the wealthiest teenager in history," with more

Marigny Family Tomb

than enough assets to live out the rest of his life lavishly, yet he ended up destitute and terribly in debt, renting a two-room residence in a boarding house on Frenchman Street, and at age 53 had to go to work as a clerk in the Office of Mortgages and Conveyances after having been not only a business tycoon but also a senator who helped frame the state constitution.

Whether by gambling, bad business deals, extreme generosity, wild living, or an estranged and litigious wife, Bernard de Marigny knew how to go through money. This tendency was instilled into him during his upbringing. For example, at age thirteen Bernard witnessed his father lend money to the future king of France, Duke of Orleans Louis-Philippe, great-great-grandson of the city's namesake. The future king had been in the United States avoiding the French Revolution, and while in Louisiana was a Marigny houseguest. The Marignys held a reception for him during which they ate off gold, and figured this event was so important that they could never use that gold again. They would then throw those golden plates into the Mississippi River. (Bernard de Marigny would regret this when he ended up penniless.)

Marigny was a key figure in Louisiana's transition from French to American, having participated in the framing of the first and second state constitutions, serving in the Louisiana territorial legislature, and being elected president of the state senate. As a politician, his personal style appealed to the French Creoles. This appeal was evident during a political campaign when an American opponent attacked him for being a womanizer and he countered by asking his constituency if New Orleans wanted to eliminate its taste for love. French New Orleans sided with him, just as today's French scoff at the American political system's and media's obsession with the private lives of office-holders.

Marigny's most enduring legacy can be found in the streets of New Orleans. In a city renowned for curious street names, he dubbed far more than any one person. While going bankrupt Bernard sold off his plantation to create the residential "Marigny" section and he named streets after his favorite things. Naturally there was a Craps St., and one named Pleasure, Benifit, and Treasure. Abundance, Music, Humanity, Poets, Duels, Peace, History, and Elysian Fields were his ideas. He named a street Desire, for which the Streetcar-Named-Desire line was named.

Marigny's street name "Desire" gave rise to a metaphor which serves as the basis for one of the greatest American plays ever written. Interestingly, Tennessee Williams used to enjoy visiting the City of the Dead, finding inspiration here. (He actually requested to be buried in the St. Louis #1, but ended up buried in St. Louis, Missouri.) Yet Williams did not fully exploit Bernard de Marigny's imaginative street-naming. Next to Desire Street Marigny placed a Piety Street. Desire-and-Piety-running-side-by-side is a humorous yet truthful fixture of New Orleans streets with which it seems Tennessee Williams could have had a field day. (Today the defunct street-car's route is serviced by a bus, called Desire.)

And then there was Love St., named for a zone which was home to many quadroon mistresses. Marriage of wealthy Creoles was often nothing more than a combination of two large fortunes; love was frequently found in the mistress, a tradition tragic and subsequently romanticized. Louisiana was not the only colony where wealthy men kept mistresses of mixed race, but here these ladies were treated relatively better. They were given homes and the children often received paternal surnames, full inheritance, and education. Whereas many communities would shun such offspring, New Orleans had scores living on a street which Marigny named, "La Rue des Bons Enfants," the Street of Good Children. This street is now part of St. Claude Avenue, but Marigny's sensibilities still identify many New Orleans streets, streets known the world over as "outdoor museums."

Courtesy Historic New Orleans Collection

"They told me to take a streetcar named Desire and then transfer to one called Cemeteries and ride six blocks and get off at — Elysian Fields."
— Blanche DuBois, "with faintly hysterical humor," from the opening scene of Tennessee Williams' *A Streetcar Named Desire*.[12]

The Protestant Section

As you walk along the rear path of the cemetery, you are in the shadow of the oldest wall vault in Louisiana. Few plaques remain, but the few that tenaciously cling to the wall indicate a striking geographical diversity: natives of Bordeaux, France; St. Domingue (Haiti); Czechoslavakia ("One of the greatest violin masters of the South"); Cuba; and Hydra, Greece. As in New Orleans itself, much cultural diversity in the City of the Dead is achieved through geographical diversity. A multitude of countries feeds this cemetery: Portugal, Senegal, Spain, Malta, Martinique, Italy, Ireland, and the Congo.

The diversity of this cemetery transcends geography. Every walk of life that has called New Orleans home rests here: the richest of the rich (i.e., the Marigny Family) and the poorest of the poor (i.e., paupers, and Bernard de Marigny); Creoles and immigrants; slaves and free people of color; veterans from every war in which New Orleanians have participated, starting with the American Revolution. Movers and shakers, downtrodden and destitute, celebrated and anonymous—every imaginable type of New Orleanian is herein entombed.

Oldest bank of wall vaults in Louisiana

However, this cemetery did separate people in one way: religion. Colonial Louisiana was Roman Catholic by law, and the Archdiocese has always owned and managed the St. Louis #1. The church did not actively prevent the few non-Catholic colonial New Orleanians from being buried in the St. Louis #1, and most of them would marry Catholics with family tombs anyway. But after the Louisiana Purchase, when thousands of Protestant Americans flooded New Orleans, a "Protestant Section" was assigned to Christ Episcopal Church, at the back of the cemetery.

Upon entering the Protestant Section, you see that it is as visibly different from the Catholic section as the "American" Garden District is from the "Creole" Vieux Carre, for the newly-arrived Protestants were not prone to above-ground burial. This is curious, for their section is well below sea level. Consequently you see double layers of brick and large, heavy plaques designed to hold down the submerged coffins. With water pumping stations now draining New Orleans, a casket's potential to emerge is of little concern today. Yet legend has it that during the nineteenth century, as the water table rose, visitors to this section could hear the coffins thumping up against the top of the tombs. Although this certainly has not happened within the past century, the notion of noise-making coffins still makes people shudder.

The Protestant Section

Protestant Graves in the Water Table

The Claiborne/Lewis Family Tomb

The Protestant section is the final resting place for a number of significant non-Creole luminaries, the most noticeable tomb belonging to the family of the first American governor of Louisiana, William C. C. Claiborne of Virginia. Though the twenty-seven-year-old former Tennessee senator sent by Thomas Jefferson had just served as governor of the adjoining Mississippi Territory, accepting this position in Louisiana would in effect take him to a foreign country. Claiborne did not speak the languages. He was unfamiliar with the traditions and social customs; he was not Catholic, a significant challenge to a leader responsible for separating the church and state amongst a devoutly Catholic community. Even the climate was foreign to him.

Yet Claiborne was not in Louisiana on a vacation. He was sent not only to govern, but also to change an entrenched system. The Governor had to contend with unfamiliar law, the non-separation of church and state, rampant piracy in the Gulf of Mexico, and much more. Not only was his job strenuous, but his personal life would also suffer. This tomb reflects part of his struggle, the marble plaques clearly telling the story.

On one side of the tomb you see a plaque commemorating his wife, Eliza W. Lewis, the other side his child, Cornelia, both dying on the same day from yellow fever. In South Louisiana, one epidemic could kill thousands in a matter of weeks. On the back of the tomb you see a plaque for his brother-in-law, Micajah Green Lewis, dying in a duel defending the governor's honor. Where Claiborne came from dueling was not a day to day occurrence; in New Orleans it was a social institution. (Claiborne himself would stumble into a very embarrassing duel with a man now buried only a few paces away from his tomb. Dueling in New Orleans always had strong connections with the cities of the dead. As a matter of fact, New Orleans most successful duelist, Jose "Pepe" Lula, would operate his own cemetery.)

Claiborne later married a local girl, Clarice Duralde, who was Catholic. Her family tomb is just over the boundary of the Catholic section. The second Mrs. Claiborne is therefore buried right across the way from Claiborne's first wife. Governor Claiborne himself was entombed here but in 1880 was given a second funeral and then moved to the Metairie Cemetery.

Claiborne/Lewis Family Tomb

Tomb of Clarice Duralde, second wife of Governor William Claiborne. Protestant section tomb of his first wife, Eliza Lewis, can be seen in background.

Benjamin Henry Latrobe (1764-1820)
"The Catholic tombs are very different in character from those of our Eastern and Northern cities."[13]

-Benjamin Latrobe

The designer of the Claiborne/Lewis tomb is commemorated with a plague on the adjacent wall, architect Benjamin Latrobe. Nationally acclaimed, Latrobe was responsible for such structures as the Baltimore Cathedral, the Bank of Pennsylvania, and Washington D.C.'s St. John's Church and Decatur House. Through his work and that of his students, Latrobe transformed American architecture from an avocation to a profession. His influence, and his taste for Greek Revival, is so pervasive in Washington (most notably his surveying of the United States Capitol), that he almost single-handedly defined American Federal Architecture. He came to New Orleans to build a waterworks, but aside from physical structures, some of his most significant contributions to New Orleans are journal entries which give detailed accounts of the Congo Square slave gatherings.

Latrobe's sensibilities and personal impressions capture New Orleans in a cross-cultural transition following the Louisiana Purchase. Many newly arrived Americans were shocked by Creole ways, including a boisterous afternoon on the Sabbath day following Mass. One New Englander claimed, "They keep Sunday as we in Boston keep the fourth of

July!"[14] Latrobe was initially put off by this New Orleans custom, but eventually grew fond of it. In his journal, he wrote that he could "find no justification anywhere in the Bible for the strictness of the usual Protestant custom."[15]

The above-ground tombs of New Orleans were fascinating to this architect, and as he sketched and ultimately designed them, Latrobe pondered their meaning. Challenging his own deep-seated Christian beliefs, he began to question the value of burial in general, recognizing the benefits of cremation far ahead of his time. This lack of importance he placed on burial is prophetically appropriate, for the whereabouts of his own burial site remain in question.

Latrobe would die in 1820 from yellow fever and two years later, a Protestant cemetery was established on Girod Street. Many Protestants from the St. Louis #1 were moved there, and Latrobe was probably included in this exodus. In 1957 the Girod St. Cemetery was deconsecrated and demolished, the remains were moved once again to other burial grounds. It seems Latrobe became lost in the shuffle. Therefore this historic figure ends up with no tomb, rather only a plaque, perhaps quite much like he himself envisioned the future of burial.

Plaque commemorating Architect Benjamin Latrobe and son

More Catholics, Creole and Otherwise

As you re-enter the Catholic section of the cemetery, you approach two tombs containing the remains of people linked to Governor Claiborne: the second Mrs. Claiborne, Clarice Duralde, and Daniel Clark, a man of notoriety with whom the governor fought a duel. Clark, a wealthy Irish-born merchant, was American consul to Louisiana prior to the Louisiana Purchase. He has been credited with persuading Thomas Jefferson to execute history's greatest real estate deal. Daniel Clark was later territorial delegate to Congress, but in terms of political endeavor, he is most well-remembered in New Orleans for a scandal. (Imagine that . . .)

Clark was accused of being part of the Aaron Burr Conspiracy. It is believed that Burr (former Vice President of the United States and killer of Alexander Hamilton in a duel) crafted a scheme in which he intended to take parts of Louisiana and Texas and to annex them with parts to Mexico. Obviously this never happened, but the threat was taken quite seriously, for Burr was in league with some powerful people. Daniel Clark was one such accused conspirator.

Governor Claiborne issued a warrant for Clark's arrest. Clark responded by challenging the governor to a duel. In other parts of the United States at that time, it would have been a joke to challenge a governor to a duel, but not in Louisiana. Claiborne had to accept this challenge or he would have lost face with his newly acquired territory. And on top of the indignity of having to agree to a duel, Claiborne lost. Adding injury to insult, he was shot in the leg during this public duel. Such were the occupational hazards of his new job.

Myra Clark Gaines (1803-1885)

Buried in the same single-tiered family tomb is a daughter of Clark's, Myra Clark Gaines. Her commemorative plaque reads: "Daughter of Daniel Clark and Zulime Carriere." Throughout most of their lives, this couple was assumed to be childless and unmarried. Zulime Carriere was initially Daniel Clark's mistress. Her unwed pregnancy coincided with the Louisiana Purchase. Since Clark feared that a scandal could jeopardize his involvement in the Purchase, he enlisted a business associate to raise the child. Ultimately, Zulime Carriere and Daniel Clark were married, but not until after a convoluted real-life soap opera was played out.

Myra Clark Gaines
Courtesy The Historic New Orleans Collection

One obstacle to their marriage had been the fact that Zulime Carriere was also married to someone else, Jerry des Grange. She found a way out of that marriage upon learning that Des Grange had married another woman in Philadelphia. Carriere went there to investigate, and even though the church where her husband was remarried had burned to the ground, and the priest who conducted the wedding was dead, she got proof of the marriage. Daniel Clark showed up in Philadelphia that same weekend and he married Zulime Carriere secretly. So secretly, it seems, that the two of them themselves forgot about it and were either married or engaged to someone else within a couple of years.

The fact that they were legally married ended up being significant for Myra Clark Gaines. In Louisiana, under a system of civil law, there exists the legal doctrine of "forced heirship," meaning that estates must stay in families. Daniel Clark had amassed a tremendous amount of real estate, yet the night before Clark died, his will inexplicably disappeared. However, Clark's business partners came up with a second-to-last will which named themselves as the beneficiaries and no heirs contested. At that time, Myra did not know that she was an heir. But at age twenty-five, she discovered all the unusual circumstances behind her birth and under the doctrine of forced heirship would embark upon the longest law suit in American history.

The case lasted sixty-five years, costing her $850,000 in legal fees and court costs. (The 8000 pages of court records alone cost $30,000.) After going through two entire Supreme Courts, more than thirty trial lawyers, and a couple of husbands, Myra was ultimately determined to be Daniel Clark's legal heir. Even with "forced heirship" on her side, she never claimed any of her father's estate. She herself was drained, financially and emotionally. Yet she acquired something she valued over and beyond any inheritance; as she herself said, "My own good name."[16] The issue had become a lifelong matter of principle, and in the end Myra Clark Gaines persevered.

Single-tiered family tomb containing historic figures
Daniel Clark and daughter Myra Clark Gaines

Etienne Boré (1741-1820)

Not far from Daniel Clark rests Etienne Boré, another historic New Orleans figure of political and business consequence, one who also crossed paths with Governor Claiborne. Boré was the city's first mayor, appointed

Tomb of Etienne Boré and his grandson, historian Charles Gayarré
Plaque bears Masonic symbol

in 1801 after France had re-acquired Louisiana from Spain. The French-speaking de Boré had to communicate with the new governor via an interpreter. The mayor's resultant frustration is believed to have contributed to his resignation six months after Claiborne's arrival.

Boré is best remembered for being the first person to successfully granulate Louisiana sugar on a commercial scale. This occurred in 1795 on his plantation (now the site of Audubon Park). Successful sugar granulation was one of the key factors behind the economic boom of antebellum New Orleans, and sugar is still one of Louisiana's major cash crops.

If you look closely at Boré's headstone, you will see something that has caught the attention of many out-of-state visitors: an inscribed Masonic symbol. Some tomb perusers are puzzled at the presence of the Masonic emblem, for you do not find Masons buried in Catholic cemeteries throughout much of the United States, and during the early nineteenth century this practice was unheard of. But Catholic Masons have always existed in New Orleans. As a matter of fact, when the Louisiana Masonic order received its charter in 1812 (the same year that Louisiana acheived American statehood), the first Grandmaster, Pierre DuBourg, was the brother of the Archbishop. It is therefore not surprising to find Freemason symbols emblazoning structures in the City of the Dead, another reflection of how pervasive Catholicism has been throughout the history of New Orleans.

The Barbarin Family Tomb

If you follow the path downriver (east), toward the Municipal Auditorium and Congo Square, you arrive at the tomb of one of New Orleans' most significant jazz dynasties, the Barbarin family. Marble plaques bear the names of musicians Izidore, Lucien, and Charles Barbarin. This tomb has probably received as many jazz funerals as any single family tomb in the city of New Orleans.

One plaque reads "Rose Barbarin Barker Colombel, My Dear Mother." She was the mother of the late guitarist/banjo player/singer/song writer/author/historian/humorist Danny Barker. Barker himself, an embodiment of so much that defines New Orleans's music, is not buried here, for there have been no recent burials in this tomb. It is victim to a common occurrence which discourages burial in some older tombs, the fact that some old vaults are not big enough to accommodate today's larger caskets. Danny is therefore buried in a St. Louis Cemetery #2 tomb belonging to his uncle, the late drummer Paul Barbarin.

Barbarin Family Tomb

Danny Barker was highly revered as a profound link to the past who perpetuated Traditional Jazz until nearly the twenty-first century. This man who played with Jelly Roll Morton and Louis Armstrong would become a driving force behind the recent New Orleans brass band revival. Barker was a strong and crucial keeper of tradition, and he considered the jazz funeral to be an invaluable institution in dire need of sustaining. Danny Barker became associated with the jazz funeral not only as musician and cultural preservationist, but also due to his characteristically humorous commentary and antics.

For example, Danny would actively spread the word of a friend's jazz funeral, on one occasion publicly announcing that there would be free food and whiskey. This claim was not true, but was meant to ensure good attendance. In his book, *A Life in Jazz*, he writes, "Tourists who repeat trips to New Orleans always ask jazzmen when, or if there is a jazz funeral scheduled. Then there is the jazzmen's comic reply, 'No, there's no funeral that we know or hear of today or tomorrow, but if you have enough money we can arrange one—get some cat killed.' That always gets a laugh."[17] (A travel magazine recently printed a story which listed the most ridiculous tourist questions imaginable; the list included people who plan trips to New Orleans and call a year in advance to ask for a schedule of next season's jazz funerals.)

In his own classic adaptation of "St. James Infirmary," Danny Barker sang:

> "When I die I want you to dress me in straight-laced shoes
> Put my shoes on because I may have to run from the devil
> I want a box back coat and a Stetson hat
> Put my hat on because the cinders and
> the fire will be falling
> Put a twenty dollar gold piece on my watch chain
> So all my phony whiskey-head reefer-head friends
> will know I passed away standing pat (have mercy. . .)
>
> I want sixteen snow white horses - no mules, no ponies, no jackasses -
> all horses
> Sixteen chorus girls from the Apollo Theatre to sing and dance me a
> song
> Put a jazz band on the top of my casket
> To blow the Memphis Blues as they slowly stroll along."[18]

New Orleans was therefore taken aback when prior to his death, Barker stated that he did not want a jazz funeral. He claimed that the tradition had

Danny Barker's Jazz Funeral, en route to St. Louis Cemetery #2
Photo by Pat Jolly

deteriorated into a rowdy spectacle. "They make a mockery of funerals now,"[19] Barker told writer Jason Berry. However, New Orleans musicians pleaded the need for a jazz funeral to his wife, the legendary singer Blue Lu Barker. She agreed, but only after being guaranteed that the procession would stay dignified, and dignified it was.

Paul Morphy (1837-1884)

Toward the gate of the cemetery lie the remains of another internationally significant figure, Paul Morphy, America's most undisputed chess champion. This native New Orleanian won his first public match at the age of nine, beating General Winfield Scott of Virginia, the strategist

Paul Morphy at work
Courtesy Louisiana State Museum

who masterminded the Union Army's defeat of the Confederacy. At age thirteen he would defeat a former world-reigning chess champion, A. J. Lowenthal of Hungary.

Having finished law school by age twenty, Morphy went to New York to compete in the Chess Congress; he was victorious in ninety-seven of one hundred games, taking first prize. The next year he defeated Europe's premiere chess players. At the remarkably young age of twenty-one he left a sickbed to defeat the reigning world champion, Adolph Anderson of Germany. Morphy then took on tremendous significance in his own country.

During the mid-nineteenth century, while developing a national character and outlook, a young United States was suffering from an identity crisis, if not an inferiority complex. Ralph Waldo Emerson complained about a "want of self culture,"[19] lamenting that the American spirit, through religion, education, and art, looked abroad. In "The American Scholar," he wrote, "Our day of dependence, our long apprenticeship to the learning of other lands, draws to a close."[20] Morphy answered his call.

Oliver Wendell Holmes declared Morphy "a triumph of the American intellect,"[21] celebrating the rapid rate at which Americans had learned "to outrun, outsail, and checkmate the rest of Creation."[22] Yet Morphy was not ultimately overjoyed. Feeling a champion's inevitable lack of challenge, he retired at the age of twenty-two, never to play another game of competitive chess. His life would then go into a downward spiral.

Morphy was denied a diplomatic assignment at the beginning of the Civil War. By the time of the occupation the Morphy family had fled to Cuba, and then proceeded to Paris, a city where Paul had been celebrated in victory. At this point his mind began to slip, progressively worsening throughout the rest of his life. Following the war, he became delusional, believing that people wanted to kill him.

On one occasion Morphy tried to publicly assault a close friend with his walking stick. At times he was overheard on his verandah cryptically muttering in French, "He will plant the banner of Castille upon the walls of Madrid, amidst the cries of the conquered city, and the little king will go away looking very sheepish."[23] Although he would die a tragic shadow of his former self, chess enthusiasts to this day make pilgrimages to the Morphy tomb. Some leave chess boards at the foot of the tomb, upon which are placed winning moves of Paul Morphy's great games.

Speaking of pilgrimages, the grave across from Morphy's is an absolute shrine: the tomb of Marie Laveau.

Paul Morphy Tomb

Marie Laveau (c.1794-1881)

Marie Laveau was the reigning Voodoo priestess of the nineteenth century. New Orleans Voodoo as a social phenomenon came into its heyday during the 1800s. Under Marie Laveau's guidance Voodoo thrived as a business, served as a form of political influence, provided a source or spectacle and entertainment, and was a means of altruism. But what Voodoo is in its pure form is religion: forms of worship brought to Caribbean and American colonies through the slave trade.

Due to slavery, the entire life of the transplanted African was tragically altered. Naturally the religious beliefs and practices would change. This mutation of West African religion under the strain of slavery ultimately gave rise to the New-World phenomenon known as "Voodoo." More than any one person, Marie Laveau transformed the religious practices of African slaves into a major social and cultural institution of nineteenth-century New Orleans. On many levels, her life was an embodiment of New Orleans Voodoo.

To begin with, New Orleans Voodoo is steeped in Catholicism. Marie Laveau, the most renowned Voodoo figure in the history of North America, has been buried in a Catholic cemetery which has a separate section for Protestants. She was a devout Catholic who attended Mass at the St. Louis Cathedral nearly every day. First public record of her appears at the Cathedral, where she was married to Jacque Paris on August 4, 1819. To a greater extent than her predecessors, Marie Laveau would mix holy water, Catholic prayers, incense, and saints into the African-based Voodoo rites.

New Orleans Voodoo, like New Orleans culture, is a mixture. Marie Laveau herself was a mixture: She was a free person of color, born to Charles Laveau, a wealthy French planter, and a mother who sources indicate could have been a mulatto slave, a Caribbean Voodoo practitioner, or a quadroon mistress. Marie may also have been part Choctaw. The objects and actions employed in the practice of New Orleans Voodoo are called "gris-gris". "Gris" is the French word for grey, signifying a mixture of black and white magic, magic which can be used for different purposes. Gris-gris, the basis of New Orleans Voodoo practice, is a concept which is based upon mixture.

Marie Laveau's gender is indicative of New Orleans Voodoo. Hers was a matriarchal sect, like the African religion upon which it is based. Marie Laveau also embodies New Orleans Voodoo as an impresario. Voodoo ceremonies in Marie Laveau's day were looked upon by some people as entertainment; she was the one who introduced this show-biz element. She

Marie Laveau, Voodoo Queen
Courtesy Louisiana State Museum

understood theatrical staging, possessing a good sense of what people would line up and pay to see. These performances, and her general voodoo practice, were highly lucrative. Aspects of nineteenth-century New Orleans Voodoo were also business-oriented, and she was a consummate business-woman.

Marie Laveau could very well be the person who eternally solidified the connection between the City of New Orleans and the practice of Voodoo. But despite her historic significance, much confusion surrounds her life, and this tomb. For example, the commemorative plaque states that this is the "reputed" burial place of this woman. Some of the information on the headstone corresponds with what is known about her: Marie, nee 'Laveau', marries carpenter Jacques Paris. He dies within six years and she has become the "Widow Paris". She thereafter became common-law wife to ship captain Christopher Glapion, who had distinguished himself in the Battle of New Orleans. The names Laveau, Paris and Glapion are all accounted for on this family tomb.

Yet the date of death, 1897, is not hers, but closer to her daughter's, Marie Laveau II. So the question is, which one of them is buried here? Some say they were both buried in this tomb; others believe neither are here. Many people think their remains were switched between the St. Louis #1 and #2 cemeteries. The answer to this question is unclear and perpetually debated, as there are endless discrepancies in recorded information about her, much of it being legend. Yet even if Marie Laveau had been buried here, her remains would not necessarily be inside. Since bones are one of the most popular forms of gris-gris, it is likely that a Voodoo practitioner cleared them out of the vault shortly after her entombment.

In a sense, it does not really matter if Marie Laveau was buried here, because the tomb has been accepted as her final resting place and for generations the devoted and the curious have been visiting this site, conducting all kinds of rituals, leaving all kinds of gris-gris. You never quite know what you will find upon visiting this gravesite, anything from a wedding cake couple circled in coconut, cayenne, and honey, to a freshly dead rat wearing Mardi Gras beads.

But you will always find innumerable "X"'s blanketing this tomb and several others. The orgins of this proverbial New Orleans Voodoo practice are unclear, but contrary to popular belief, it is not rooted in age-old local ritual. Judging from the sheer amount of X's scrawled throughout the cemetery, it would appear that legions of Voodoo practitioners make their way through the City of the Dead on a regular basis. Although more

Voodoo is practiced at this one tomb than any single tomb in the United States, many people who worship through Voodoo and genuinely live it as a lifestyle have never left a mark on the structures of the City of the Dead.

The thousands of X's are largely the result of tour groups, who have paid to learn how to practice Voodoo. Their instructions always include breaking brick off of other tombs (notice the neighboring tombs depleted of their bricks) and a combination of steps which involve spinning around three times, scratching three X's on the tomb, knocking on it or rubbing a foot on it or hollering at it or kicking it, etc. (everyone does it slightly, if not very, differently from everyone else) and then leaving an offering to get a wish granted.

So is this or is this not New Orleans Voodoo? It is, in that there is no doctrine or reasonable dictionary definition of Voodoo. Practitioners create ritual as they practice. However, the Glapion family who owns the tomb does not call this "Voodoo" but rather "vandalism," and have complained that they can no longer read the inscriptions through what one family member considers "graffiti." There are also tourist brochures and hotel concierges instructing wish seekers to scratch three X's on her tomb, and even travel books which recommend the practice. But one of the most striking accounts of this practice appeared in a major supermarket tabloid, the story of a woman winning two million dollars in the Missouri State lottery after scratching X's on Marie Laveau's tomb.

Glapion Family Tomb

Amanda Carroll/Arthur Smith

Around the corner from Marie Laveau waits an even more glaring example of how suspect the X-scrawling can be. On the bank of wall vaults, close to the front gate, you will find a family vault bearing an enlarged, multi-colored photocopy of a woman, Amanda Boswell Carroll. Frequently found above this image are many X's. Tour guides can be heard explaining that she was "the great Voodoo priestess of the 1930s and 40s." Some even announce that the portrait depicts Marie Laveau herself.

Amanda Carroll was no Voodoo practitioner, but rather the grandmother of Arthur Smith. Mr. Smith is the one who periodically changes the

"As sure as the sun is shining, I know she's smiling down on us. . . ."
says Arthur Smith of grandmother Amanda Boswell Carroll.

picture and decorates the tomb as a shrine to this woman who helped raise him. He claims that the tomb's significance in the overall cemetery scheme is not Voodoo-related, but rather lies in it's inscription slab bearing the only photographic image in the cemetery aside from that of the late Mayor Morial, and because this curious grave has been photographed by countless thousands of people from the four corners of the world.

When guides instruct visitors to scratch X's on the Amanda Carroll tomb, they are therefore defacing historic property, spreading incorrect information, and charging money for that service. But the most damaging effect comes in offending the families who own the tombs. (Arthur Smith rails at such desecration, calling it "highly disrespectful.") The bottom line is that not everything with X's scrawled on it has anything to do with Voodoo whatsoever.

Yet despite these questionable practices, the tomb of Marie Laveau has always been viewed as the most significant site for New Orleans Voodoo practice, and is consequently the most famous tomb in the state of Louisiana.

Ernest "Dutch" Morial (1929-1989)

As you gaze about the St. Louis Cemetery #1, it is easy to feel that you are standing amidst a relic. In some ways you are. With an average twenty-five burials a year here, much of the cemetery has fallen into disrepair from lack of use. Yet the cemetery is by no means ancient history. Due to "forced heirship," many nineteenth-century tombs are currently owned by old New Orleans families, some of considerable historic significance.

Consider Marie Laveau. Family historian Walter Glapion believes that every Glapion in the New Orleans phone book is connected to her. And today there are some high profile Glapions, such as Gail Glapion, current Orleans Parish School Board member, who has acknowledged a family belief that they are somehow linked to Marie. But speaking of old Creole families and politics, many find it interesting that buried right next to Marie Laveau is Dutch Morial, the city's first African-American mayor.

Dutch Morial left a long list of political firsts. Aside from being New Orleans' first black mayor, he was the first black judge, the first elected to the Louisiana House of Representatives, the first black to graduate from L.S.U law school, and founded New Orleans's first black-owned bank. His far-reaching legacy lives in the New Orleans political arena today, not only

Funeral of Dutch Morial. His wife Sybil is comforted by their sons Marc and Jacques. After a jazz funeral attended by thousands, the last rites are conducted by Archbishop Phillip Hannan as family and friends, including Jesse Jackson, pay their last respects. The Morial family tomb has since been renovated.
Photo by A. J. Sisco

The late Mayor Dutch Morial entombed right next to Marie Laveau

in policy established and coalitions formed, but also in a more immediate way: his son Marc Morial is now the mayor of New Orleans, elected at age thirty-six. Marc Morial was quickly reminiscent of his father. Early in his term, the *Times-Picayune* wrote, "The young mayor Morial has reminded many of his father, former Mayor Dutch Morial: ready to take a tough stand on a matter of principle and not back down until he's secured most of his demands."[25]

So is this cemetery ancient history? Absolutely not. When you consider who in the present and future could be laid to rest here, it is clear that the St. Louis Cemetery #1 is still on the cutting edge of New Orleans history and culture. This City of the Dead indeed evokes life, offering a final resting place to a city which never truly rests, a place forever beckoned by its past.

Epilogue

Most visitors are fascinated by the City of the Dead, yet some are puzzled over how parts of it have fallen into such disrepair. To begin with, the cemetery is more than two hundred years old. Responsibility for tombs falls on individuals and families. Several have died off or moved away, and the burial societies responsible for the society tombs no longer exist. Unless one has "perpetual care," a tomb is left to do battle with the elements. With St. Louis Cemetery #1 receiving significantly fewer burials than in the past, it receives less money that goes towards maintenance, and there are fewer visitors sprucing up their family tombs and the surrounding area. This tendency creates a self-perpetuating cycle.

Above-ground tombs are an expensive investment, and people are less inclined to place family members for perpetuity in one surrounded by decay. The inverse of this trend is true. The overall condition of the St. Louis Cemetery #3 is impressive, because there is a waiting list to occupy its tombs. But with less income, the oldest city of the dead deteriorates more rapidly.

This creates a vicious cycle, a major and dangerous way in which this city of dead reflects the City of New Orleans, or the dynamics of any present day American city: People move away from the city's undesirable conditions and revenues diminish; with less money the city's quality of life decreases and more people flee.

Lack-of-use translating into lack-of-maintenance has much to do with the cemetery's current crisis. But this dilemma is not unique to St. Louis #1. There are cemeteries throughout the country which suffer from neglect, as well as historic sites throughout the world in an identical predicament. A fitting parallel is seen at the ancient theatres of the Parthenon. The Theatre of Dionysus, whose festivals gave birth to the theatrical tradition by producing the plays of Aeschylus and Sophocles, is strewn with weeds and seemingly abandoned, as it is no longer being used. Yet the neighboring Odeon of Herodes Atticus, is in fine restored condition, because it is used for performances.

A ray of encouragement recently arrived at the City of the Dead, Perry Mathieu, assigned by the Archdiocese as sexton of the St. Louis #1 and #2 cemeteries. Mr. Mathieu formerly did a magnificent job maintaining the St. Roch Cemetery, one of the city's most dazzling and cleanest graveyards. He now turns not only his skill and attention but also his enthusiastic concern toward St. Louis Cemetery, a place he refers to as "the crown jewel of New

Funerals

Renovation and Construction of Tombs
Johnson/Febres Tomb

Orleans." Several weeks after his arrival, the burial ground had improved immensely.

However, complete salvation of the world-renowned New Orleans cemeteries may be beyond the staff of the Archdiocese, or historic preservation groups, or government agencies. Perhaps *use* is the only thing which can effectively save abandoned historic sites. (Lately, cemetery restoration has been increasing. A long overdue trend may have been inspired by the recent tomb acquisition on the parts of artist George Febres and historian Jerah Johnson, the first private transfer of St. Louis #1 property in many years. Many people are also now realizing that their great, great grandfather's tomb could save them thousands of dollars.) Similarly, the most effective means of reviving an abandoned city is residence. This is the most pressing and profound way in which the city of the dead now reflects the City of New Orleans. If New Orleans is to be saved from decay, it needs to be reclaimed and resided in. The same can be said for the St. Louis Cemetery #1.

On the other hand, there are many who would argue that this very decay brings life to the cities of the dead, that therein lies much of the mysterious and brilliant, unplanned aesthetic quality.

TOUR ROUTE

Bear in mind that you are responsible for yourself in the St. Louis Cemetery. The Archdiocese has posted a plaque that reads as follows:

VISITORS ARE WELCOME BUT ENTER THESE PREMISES AT THEIR OWN RISK. NO SECURITY NOR GUARDS ARE PROVIDED AND THE NEW ORLEANS ARCHDIOCESAN CEMETERIES DISCLAIMS RESPONSIBILITY FOR THE PERSONAL SAFETY OF VISITORS AND THEIR PROPERTY.

TREME STREET

(Lakeside)

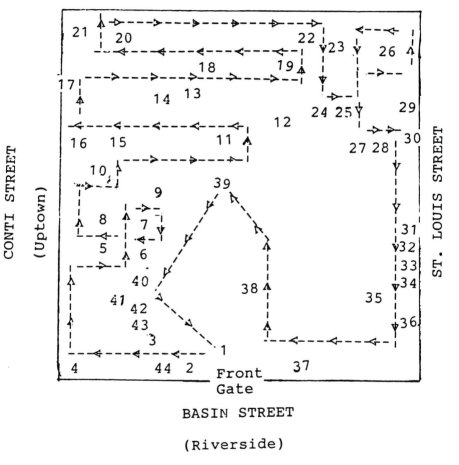

BASIN STREET

(Riverside)

Tour Map Stops

1. Varney Tomb, p. 13
2. Wall Vaults/Oven Vaults, p. 16 & plaque
3. The Family Tomb, p. 19
4. View from front to back.
5. Stepped Tomb, p. 25
6. Society Tombs/New Ladies Hope B.A.
7. Italian Society Tomb, p. 27 & plaque
8. Portuguese/St. Vincent Society Tomb, p. 30 & plaque
9. Portuguese Society Tomb & plaque
10. Cervantes/Spanish Society Tomb, p. 31 & plaque
11. Orleans Battalion of Artillery Tomb, p. 33 & plaque
12. Archdiocesan marble & iron exhibit, plaque
13. French Society Tomb, p. 31
14. Chinese Society Tomb, p. 31
15. Cemetery Furniture, p. 23
16. Homer Plessy Tomb, p. 35
17. Marigny Family Tomb, p. 35
18. Oldest Louisiana wall vault, p. 44 & plaque
19. Protestant Section, p. 45 & plaque
20. Confederate Brig. Gen. John Grayson
21. Layton Tomb, plaque
22. Claiborne/Lewis Tomb, p. 47 & plaque
23. Latrobe plaque, p. 49
24. Clarice Duralde Tomb, p. 48 & plaque
25. Daniel Clark & Myra Clark Gaines Tomb, p. 52 & plaque
26. Back corner, excellent iron & marble, plaque
27. Table-top style monument
28. De Bore Tomb, p. 53 & plaque
29. Barbarin Family Tomb, p. 55
30. Febres/Johnson Tomb, p. 69
31. Dieu Nous Protege Society Tomb
32. Blaise Cenas Tomb, plaque
33. Louis Moreau Lislet Tomb, plaque
34. Carlos Trudeau Tomb, plaque
35. Michel Fortier Tomb, plaque
36. Wall vault of Mediteranean immigrants
37. Buddy Ansbacker Tomb, plaque
38. Grima Family Tomb, plaque
39. Pierre Derbigny Tomb, plaque
40. Henry Dick Tomb, plaque
41. Paul Morphy Tomb, p. 59 & plaque
42. Marie Laveau Tomb, p. 63 & plaque
43. Morial Family Tomb, p. 67 & plaque
44. Amanda Carroll Tomb/Arthur Smith, p. 64

Endnotes

[1]Dennis Persica, "Repeat Floods Dog Area . . .", *New Orleans Times-Picayune*, June 15, 1995.

[2]Joan B. Garvey and Mary Lou Widmer, *The Beautiful Crescent: A History of New Orleans* (New Orleans, 1984), 33.

[3]Dr. John, "Basin St. Blues," *Goin' Back to New Orleans*, Warner Brothers Records.

[4]Al Rose, *Storyville, New Orleans* (Tuscaloosa, AL, 1974), ix.

[5]Mark Twain, *Life on the Mississippi* (New York, 1990), 199.

[6]Norman C. Ferachi and Sue L. Eakin, *Vanishing Louisiana* (Baton Rouge, 1977), 12.

[7]Anne Rice, *Interview With the Vampire*, Katherine Ramsland, *Prism of the Night* (New York, 1992), 183.

[8]Keith Weldon Medley, quoted from *The Smithsonian Magazine*, February 1994.

[9]James MacGregor Burns and Stuart Burns, *A Peoples Charter: The Pursuit of Rights in America* (New York, 1991), 133.

[10]Arnold R. Hirsch and Joseph Logsdon, eds., *Creole New Orleans: Race and Americanization* (Baton Rouge, 1992), 195.

[11]Leavitt, *Great Characters of New Orleans*, 83.

[12]Tennessee Williams, *A Streetcar Named Desire* (New York, 1947), Act I Sc i.

[13]Leonard V. Huber, Peggy McDowell, and Mary Louise Christovich, *New Orleans Architecture: The Cemeteries* (Gretna, LA, 1989), 73.

[14]Lilian Crete, *Daily Life in Louisiana: 1815-1830* (Baton Rouge, 1981), 71.

[15]Talbot Hamlin, *Benjamin Henry Latrobe* (New York, 1955), 517.

[16]Myra Clark Gaines, quoted from Leavitt, *Great Characters of New Orleans*, 31.

[17]Danny Barker, *A Life in Jazz* (New York, 1986), 49.

[18]Danny Barker, "St. James Infirmary," *Save the Bones*, Orleans Records.

[19]Danny Barker, *The Catholic Reporter*, April 1, 1994.

[20]Ralph Waldo Emerson, "Self-Reliance," quoted from Ronald Gottesman, ed., *The Norton Anthology of American Literature* (New York, 1980), 316.

[21]Emerson, "The American Scholar," ibid., 270.

[22]Oliver Wendell Holmes, quoted from Leavitt, *Great Characters of New Orleans*, 78.

[23]Ibid., 79.

[24]David Lawson, *Paul Morphy, The Pride and Sorrow of Chess* (New York, 1976), 299.

[25]Bruce Eggler and Frank Donze, *New Orleans Times-Picayune*, July 15, 1994.

Bibliography

Archdiocese of New Orleans: *Our Lady of Guadalupe Chapel.*

Archdiocesan Plaques in St. Louis Cemetery #1.

Archeology News: "Uncovered French Quarter Burials Analyzed," April 1986, Vol. 3, No. 1.

Barker, Danny. *A Life in Jazz.* New York/Oxford: Oxford University Press, 1986.

Berry, Jason. "Eastery Funeral Liturgy Sets a Jazz Legend Loose," National Catholic Reporter, April 1, 1994.

Bodin, Ron. *Voodoo: Past and Present.* Lafayette, LA: The Center for Louisiana Studies, 1990.

Burns, James MacGregor, and Burns, Stuart. *A Peoples Charter: The Pursuit of Rights in America.* New York: Knopf, 1991.

Carey, Joseph S. *Your Cemetery Plot and Title.* New Orleans, LA: St. Louis Catholic Cathedral, 1948.

Carter, Hodding. *Past as Prelude: New Orleans, 1718-1968.* Gretna, LA: Pelican Books, 1968.

Chase, John Churchill. *Frenchmen, Desire, Goodchildren, and Other Streets of New Orleans.* New York: Collier Books, 1979.

De Conde, Alexander. *This Affair of Louisiana.* New York: Charles Scribner's Sons, 1976.

Fonda, Peter, Hopper, Dennis, and Southern, Terry. *Easy Rider: Original Screenplay.* New York: Signet Books, 1969.

The Gambit, Blake Pontchartrain letter, May 23, 1995.

Gandolfo, Henri A., *Metairie Cemetery: An Historical Memoir.* New Orleans, LA: Stewart Enterprises, Inc., 1981.

Garvey, Joan B., and Widmer, Mary Lou. *Beautiful Crescent: A History of New Orleans*. New Orleans, LA: Garmer Press, Inc., 1984.

Gehman, Mary. *The Free People of Color of New Orleans: An Introduction*. New Orleans, LA: Margaret Media, Inc., 1994.

Gehman, Mary. *Women and New Orleans*. New Orleans, LA: Margaret Media, Inc., 1985.

Hall, Gwendolyn Midlo. *Africans in Colonial Louisiana*. Baton Rouge, LA: Louisiana State University Press, 1992.

Hamlin, Talbot. *Benjamin Henry Latrobe*. New York: Oxford University Press, 1955.

Harmon, Nolan Bailey. *The Famous Case of Myra Clark Gaines*. Baton Rouge: Louisiana State University Press, 1946.

Hirsch, Arnold R., and Logsdon, Joseph, eds., *Creole New Orleans: Race and Americanization*. Baton Rouge, LA: Louisiana State University Press, 1992.

Huber, Leonard V., McDowell, Peggy, and Christovich, Mary Louise. *New Orleans Architecture: The Cemeteries*. Gretna, LA: Pelican Publishing Company, 1989.

Janssen, James S. *Building New Orleans: The Engineer's Role*. New Orleans, LA: Waldemar S. Nelson & Company, 1984.

Laughlin, C. J. "Cemeteries of New Orleans," *Architectural Review*, February, 1948.

Lawson, David. *The Pride and Sorrow of Chess*. New York: McKay, 1976.

Leavitt, Mel. *Great Characters of New Orleans*. San Francisco, Ca.: Lexicos, 1984.

Lofgren, Charles A. *The Plessy Case*. New York: Oxford University Press, 1987.

Maddux, Dianne, ed., *Master Builders*. Washington DC: Preservation Press, 1985.

Medley, Keith Weldon. "The Sad Story of How 'Separate-but-Equal' was Born." Smithsonian Magazine, February, 1994.

Meyer, Richard E., ed., *Cemeteries and Gravemakers: Voices of American Culture*. Ann Arbor, Mi.: U.M.I. Research Press, 1989.

Olsen, Otto H., ed., *The Thin Disguise: Turning Point in Negro History, Plessy vs. Ferguson*. New York: Humanities Press, 1967.

Rose, Al. *Storyville, New Orleans*. Tuscaloosa, Alabama: The University of Alabama Press, 1974.

Saxon, Lyle; Dreyer, Edward, and Tallant, Robert. *Gumbo Ya-Ya*. Gretna, LA: Pelican Publishing Company, 1991.

Tallant, Robert. *Voodoo in New Orleans*. Gretna, LA: Pelican Publishing Company, 1983.

Veigle, Anne. "Bones Will Give Clues to Lifestyle in 19th Century," *New Orleans Times Picayune*, February 22, 1987.

Voiter, Regina. *The Life of Paul Morphy in The Vieux Carre*. New Orleans Publications, 1926.

Wilson, Samuel, Jr., & Huber Leonard V. *The St. Louis Cemeteries of New Orleans*. New Orleans, LA: Laborde Printing Co., 1963.

Other Sources

The Civil War Museum, New Orleans, Louisiana.

Interviews with Archdiocesan Cemetery Superintendent Michael D. Boudreaux and former Assistant Director Ivan Foley.

Jerah Johnson, Historian.

Janice Lee. Internment Coordinator at Metairie Cemetery, Lakelawn Park, and Mt. Olivet Cemetery.

Louisiana State Museum exhibit entitled, "Disease, Death, and Mourning."

Masonic Temple, Grand Secretary's Office, New Orleans, Louisiana.

National Park Service walking tours and slide presentations, Jean Lafitte National Historical Park.